POETRY FROM CRESCENT MOON

I0170186

William Shakespeare: *Selected Sonnets and Verse*
edited, with an introduction by Mark Tuley

William Shakespeare: *The Sonnets*
edited and introduced by Mark Tuley

*Shakespeare: Love, Poetry and Magic
in Shakespeare's Sonnets and Plays*
by B.D. Barnacle

Edmund Spenser: *Heavenly Love: Selected Poems*
selected and introduced by Teresa Page

Robert Herrick: *Selected Poems*
edited and introduced by M.K. Pace

Sir Thomas Wyatt: *Love For Love: Selected Poems*
selected and introduced by Louise Cooper

John Donne: *Air and Angels: Selected Poems*
selected and introduced by A.H. Ninham

D.H. Lawrence: *Being Alive: Selected Poems*
edited with an introduction by Margaret Elvy

D.H. Lawrence: Symbolic Landscapes
by Jane Foster

D.H. Lawrence: Infinite Sensual Violence
by M.K. Pace

Percy Bysshe Shelley: *Paradise of Golden Lights: Selected Poems*
selected and introduced by Charlotte Greene

Thomas Hardy: *Her Haunting Ground: Selected Poems*
edited, with an introduction by A.H. Ninham

Sexing Hardy: Thomas Hardy and Feminism
by Margaret Elvy

Emily Bronte: *Darkness and Glory: Selected Poems*
selected and introduced by Miriam Chalk

John Keats: *Bright Star: Selected Poems*
edited with an introduction by Miriam Chalk

Henry Vaughan: *A Great Ring of Pure and Endless Light: Selected Poems*
selected and introduced by A.H. Ninham

The Crescent Moon Book of Love Poetry
edited by Louise Cooper

The Crescent Moon Book of Mystical Poetry in English
edited by Carol Appleby

The Crescent Moon Book of Nature Poetry From Langland to Lawrence
edited by Margaret Elvy

The Crescent Moon Book of Metaphysical Poetry
edited and introduced by Charlotte Greene

The Crescent Moon Book of Elizabethan Love Poetry
edited and introduced by Carol Appleby

The Crescent Moon Book of Romantic Poetry
edited and introduced by L.M. Poole

Blinded By Her Light The Love-Poetry of Robert Graves
by Jeremy Mark Robinson

The Best of Peter Redgrove's Poetry: The Book of Wonders
by Peter Redgrove, edited and introduced by Jeremy Mark Robinson

Peter Redgrove: Here Comes the Flood
by Jeremy Mark Robinson

Sex-Magic-Poetry-Cornwall: A Flood of Poems
by Peter Redgrove, edited with an essay by Jeremy Mark Robinson

By-Blows: Uncollected Poems
by D.J. Enright

Petrarch, Dante and the Troubadours: The Religion of Love and Poetry
by Cassidy Hughes

Dante: *Selections From the Vita Nuova*
translated by Thomas Okey

Arthur Rimbaud: *Selected Poems*
edited and translated by Andrew Jary

Arthur Rimbaud: *A Season in Hell*
edited and translated by Andrew Jary

Jeremy Reed was born in 1951. Jeremy Reed's many poetry books include *By the Fisheries* (1984), *Nero* (1985), *Selected Poems* (1987), *Nineties* (1990) and *Kicks* (1995). Reed's books on poets include studies of Rimbaud (*Delirium: An Interpretation of Rimbaud*), *Rilke, Hopkins, Madness: The Price of Poetry and Angels, Divas and Blacklisted Heroes* (1999). Reed has translated Novalis and Montale. His novels include *The Lipstick Boys* (1984), *Blue Rock* (1987), *Isidore* (about Lautréamont), *When the Whip Comes Down* (on the Marquis de Sade), and *Chasing Black Rainbows* (1994, a fictionalized account of Antonin Artaud). His biographies include *Lou Reed, Brian Jones: The Last Decadent* (1999), *Scott Walker: Another Tear Falls* (2001) and *Marc Almond* (1999). Other books include: *St. Billie* (2001), *Sister Midnight* (1997), *Heartbreak Hotel* (2002), *The Purple Room* (2000), *Dorian* (1997), *Inhabiting Shadows* (1990), *Diamond Nebula* (1994), *Black Sugar* (1992), *Escaped Image* (1988), *Red Hot Lipstick* (1996), *The Pleasure Chateau Omnibus* (2000), *Pop Stars* (1994) and *Trucks in Camera: Bedford* (1996). Reed has won an Eric Gregory Award, the Somerset Maugham Award, and the National Poetry Competition.

Claudia Schiffer's Red Shoes

Claudia Schiffer's Red Shoes

Jeremy Reed

CRESCENT MOON

CRESCENT MOON PUBLISHING
P.O. Box 393
Maidstone
Kent, ME14 5XU
United Kingdom

First published 1998. Second edition 2008
Introduction © Jeremy Reed, 1998, 2008.

Printed and bound in Great Britain.
Set in Garamond Book 11 on 15pt.
Designed by Radiance Graphics.

British Library Cataloguing in Publication data

Reed, Jeremy
Claudia Schiffer's Red Shoes. – 2nd ed. (British Poets Series)
I. Title
821.9'14

ISBN 1-86171-149-2
ISBN-13 9781861711496

Contents

LOLITA'S BEAUTY SPOTS

Sex is a metaphor for death. She crawls
across the sofa, and you see the leaves,
a sopping, hedonistic greenblack tone
less grainy for gloss after rain
flash in the window. With her bottom up
she's reading Baudelaire, an arched proposition
gorgeously maintained. The poet said
that illness is our one democracy,
our common flavour. Wind invests the leaves
with shine, but that's incidental
to how she tastes a violet on her tongue,
each time she pits an image. What you hope
is her skirt will ride higher, as she reads
abandoned to the private ease
of no restraint on posture. Red tulips
are committing a dramatic hari-kiri,
split vulvas splashed yellow and black, CDs
are littered on the floor. Impasto leaf oblongs
keep massing on their frequency.
She stretches, and curls on one side,
and playfully imagines provoking
an eye bugging the keyhole. Poetry's
the potent aphrodisiac she needs,
and almost anticipating the next
step to enticement, pushes up her hem
and with one precocious red fingernail
pinpoints a black spot on her right buttock
and with no break, resumes reading her text.

STAR BIKINI

Rococo ceiling, converted gothic,
they took the secret with them to that place,
a hotel in the woods, a man-sized fish
guarding the lake. Had two rooms, he preferred
to imagine her late at night
undressing in a way that reminded him
of lifting petals from an artichoke.
She'd tap once on the wall to let him know
that she was almost there. Nothing but heels.

He slept beside the scarlet dress
she'd given him. She dreamt in Mexican,
brought eye to eye with petroglyphs,
the flayed god sculpted across the skyline.
She spoke the language, and forgot
the lot on waking. Later, when she kept
a recall journal, she remembered how
she'd been in the peyote dance
and lived in vision. There were storms that night
behind her eyes. They buried their secret
deeper each day, concentrated on that,
avoided words to discuss the issue,
directed thought-rays instead, finally
meditating on the white light they'd wrapped
around it as precaution. There were owls
the size of statues in the wood.
She wanted him and knocked three times that

night,
and he came in with feathers, a beaked hood.

LEOPARD SPOTTED CONDOM

Yellow bumps up, and it's forsythia
torching a statement in the windy street,
its breezy skirt split open on the wall.
A neighbourhood rivalry. What they wrote,
his novel let loose like a black dragon
slipped through the letterbox, and her at large
substantiated gay myths. She would say,
'Run your tongue three time round a cherry's rim
before you bite it. It's the sexy tang
I want my words to have.' He lit a mood
and let it smoke all week, and looking out
he hooked into a visual frame
in which forsythia was dominant.
April, arriving May. We noted things,
a dip in speech, the hope a new season
would replace summer, looked towards a night
in which pink icebergs would come sailing by
under a hazy no-month-at-all sun,
and couples sit in treetops reading how
the best ones were sent off in ships
towards a block-shaped island. But the war
continued, and our preference
in condoms changed from the clearest turquoise
to leopard spotted, a wardrobe that sex
demanded on those crazy nights when ice
nosed through with pink fins, and our need
                              advanced
in circles generated by your hips.

BLUE REMAINS

The dress over her head. It's 2 a.m.
on a day that doesn't exist,
intercalendric time, I do my nails
as poets should, a scarlet gloss,
and celebrate the unreality
of having kicked the body clock.
You stand in your bra and panties
indefinitely. There's a wind from space
delivers someone to the beach,
an arm's extended, confused contactee
arrived from missing time. The rest may still follow
converted by mutant culture.
We're free to stay for ever as we are
and be reclaimed by opportune landing
here from the nearest or the farthest star.

CLAUDIA SCHIFFER'S RED SHOES

The catwalk gives her balance. When they fix
a cocktail, it's proportionately right,
staggered for the last high-kick to the brain,
and so her body moves and asks we note

its fluency in a dark blue ensemble,
her skirt three quarters organza. What bits
of Paris did she notice in the car
in coming here to the Intercontinental,

a shop-front, a street-cleaner, a red dress,
the palette of mixed vegetables beneath
a striped awning? She tenses, and controls
the relayed fright of some imperfection

occurring on parade, and her red shoes
are packed with fidgety tension.
They'd like to run off to the Black Forest
and dance with squirrels in the fallen leaves,

I'd like to have them sit on my pillow
as prompters to lyric impulse,
spike heels overseeing the line. Backstage
she'll wait for fittings, a last rehearsal,

then reaffirm how a cocktail is mixed
to a layered consistency, no taste

preceding any other, but, hips, legs
got in one look, as she lifts floating sleeves.

CLAUDIA SCHIFFER'S BACK

The tongue imagines no impediment,
no horizontal bra strap on the back,
the spine curving to the two cantaloupes
fitted securely in black silk.
Go further. Further. I was on the stairs

listening to how rain tapped the keys
of an endlessly inconclusive text.
Stagey and smelling of red shoes, clear rain
poured like a tonic smudge in gin.
Strangely, I was expecting Marcel Proust
or the idea of him to arrive late,
purple waistcoat smoked by asthma powders.
But Claudia in a low dress tonight,
the weight of chiffon moves in a taxi
towards the pyramidal chandelier,
the paparazzi popping lights
across her cleavage, and I hold red shoes
as token loss of a last love affair.

VIRTUAL REALITY

Wetsuit and visette, he's on overkill
after a virtual Mars trip to explore
a bra-popping icon in a green pool,
a 38 cup vactor like Monroe,
or if it's legs, it's Naomi Campbell
he selects from his image reservoir.
His villa's lit in cyberspace,
the heart-shaped bed, high rococo ceilings,
jaguar bodyguards, discreet Rothkos,
an accessed, fetishistic interior
awaiting his immersion, all mirrors
to catch the sashaying celeb
in her strapless red gown, dangle-earrings,
vamping a stylised spike-heeled roll
towards the bedroom.
                    But, he half delays,
unwilling yet to visually OD
on liquid crystal screens, join the confused
who live as virtual actors with brainfade
from too much software feed. His wife, career,
are events of a fractured past;
he only earths out of necessity
to spare his eyes. Tonight he contemplates
creating himself as an arch drag queen
confronting curves stepped from a fashion shoot
into his floating life. He looks outside;
nothing has changed, a little boy
lies flat in a dappled commando suit,

his girlfriend dancing on a Daimler's roof,
dressed in the white netting of a child bride.

GREEN, RED, AND PARALLEL BLUE

It's higher up there. Thirty seven floors
clearer into the day, another time
for being different. The canvas waits
configurations, all the mineral planes
that travel at the speed of thought.
A fish gets in, a turtle shell, a bra,
the unexpected, queuing up outside,
images earning coloured tags,
I'm here and there and nowhere. Somewhere else.
I tell you that, ear that's behind my own
and Susan's, pinning up each word
to knocked on meaning. Brushes in a jar.
The possibilities someone below
might be speaking of a new poetry,
X's if he existed. I use up
my little quota of light. Learn to fly
on my dimension, polish an orange
for composition, pick the silence out
as something going one way with the sky.

LYING ON BOTH SIDES

Right to the edge. He tells her that's the place,
and points out a red curtain drawn across
the valley, side to side, and lodge to lodge –
he lives in both places, but feels no stretch,
no inherent duality. He keeps
a rhino on each property, two snakes
that sit in trees. An aircraft nosed
into the pass a month ago, and lit
a flash-fire where it crashed. He has a wife
who lives on neither side. She's in between,
so are her needs. 'If I draw the curtain,'
he reflects, 'there's a sun rises
that threatens everyone. An indigo
planet sitting on the big kill.'
He leads her back inside. The rhino waits
in its jewelled collar under trees, and dust
lifts as a full cloud from the nearest hill.

GREEN CROCHET BIKINI

The holes are burnt into my nerve linings –
the gaps, emissions, show up on the tape
fed into the pilot's black box
only to be replayed at death. I stand
under high trees, your hair dye in my coat,
a poppy coloured henna compacted
into a foil sachet. Identity.
Tomorrow, you'll be the anemone
on a thin stem I've waited for. Scarlet.
It's always odd and disproportionate
this matching of things against consciousness,
and what they mean blown up ten times life size,
no more, no less.
           Back home, you're sorting through
last summer's beachwear. It's almost autumn,
your bottom cupped by green crochet
recalls the green waters you swam last year,
sands littered all along with cowrie shells.
I catch you bent over, fishing a bra
out of the tangle. I can give you love
aimed in direction for the highest star.

GOSSARD WONDERBRA

A little conical identity,
insurgent uplift. It was green today,
by which I mean a blue and yellow sky
got in above the backdrop. On canvas,
De Chirico circa 1920,
serene juxtapositions: a statue
opens an eye in the wrong century.
You choose a black or purple bra
to offset an all over copper tan,
and then the dark arrives. A darker green.
We go by light as it instructs
a way forward out of the mind. I trap
an image, and its horns litter the small
stuff building there all day. The hook and eye
is cleanly precise, not a trick
impediment to searching hands. Laid out
the cups are top-shells. The century travels.
Circa tomorrow, and I have the map.

SHE'S NOT THERE

A blue telephone sounding in the dark.
I used to eat olives after calling
to add a salt to stimulus. The South
in imaginative geography
is sometimes North. And she's in neither place,

no dusty farm on which cactuses grow,
no white house opening to a blueblack sea
that smells of the abstract future.
And East and West where are their points in mind
I want to reach her centre all the way
and sit with her inside a sweet melon.
Instead, there's no voice answers in the night
and growing pressure in my head
that's sleeplessness, and a big spotty moth
flops on the window sucking at the light.

INCEST

It was her heels, rappy staccato stems
alerted nerve points. On the edge of sleep
he came alive imagining her shape,

a locket from behind balanced by spikes.
He knew the autumn story: a chateau
screened by the massive yellow flowering,
a boar with its tusks through the sun,
and how the boy entered his mother's room
scooped her up half dressed, unprotestingly
carried the length of three corridors
the better to enjoy her in his room,
legs arched over her head.

He heard her zip break the compact silence,
October too was a reality
with tatty orange streamers in the trees.
He stood outside the door imagining
her beach tanned figure in bra and panties,
urgent directives roaring in his veins

and went on in, and heard castrati sing.

FAST

The day resumes without the night, the day
in which the horse's tail is red roses,
a fragrant, stringy swipe at flies.
She leaves for Ecuador. 'Please don't look round,'
she asks, 'for you imagine me
as someone else, I'm terrified
I may be that person. I leave at three,
so park at five, pretend I'm there
as me, not someone else, and stay till six.'
He notices the sky he never saw,
an indigo nocturnal cube
settles above the horse. An abrupt night
is patterned with sunlit clouds, cumulus
shot through with brilliance. It's yesterday,
the time in which he should have dreamt,
but didn't. It's his mother drags a sack
through a white deserted street. She can't find
the reason for her being there, a clock
is posted on each boarded-up window.
The horse again. Its thorny tail sweeps by
in some carnival procession. A rose
falls in the dust, the scene B-sides to day,
and she is telling him, go ride the horse,
while she changes into a bikini,
a stretchy minimal black one, prepared
as always to run straight into the sea.

HOT DATES

A black sea tugs a forest window,
skeined weed, wedged as an undulating mass,
a burgundy Persian carpet.
We stand or stood beside the harbour front,
blown hair, iodine tang, a racy mood
inviting past disclosures. Where was I
when you were busy being you
as someone else? The small station
was painted green and grey you say, the year
included extra days each month,
five Tuesdays once, or a second Tuesday
in which the sea stayed blue. Now the station
is painted red and white, there's one Thursday
which seems a time spread for the beach,
like an orange towel flung over black sand.
I give you guidelines, not about my past,
but indicative of journeys,
the time I went by canoe through the trees
and found the rapids had solidified
to marble stairs. A girl and boy
were in suspension going down. We wait
for dinner at the Grand Hotel; a boat
presents light out at sea, and we walk on
into the deepening plot, across the shore,
prepared for new encounters, both certain
we'll never reach the dining room
and that we started out decades too late.

DAMAGED FISHNET

Hot seaweed jabs the nostrils, infiltrates
my overloaded nerves, I recollect
bleached damson skeins, the sea gone where
it's a blue smudge, an impacted mirage
withdrawn into a hole. Today, I miss
the curvaceous, abandoned luxury
of you in seamed fishnets, all clothes removed,
and how you'd walk about the flat like that
expecting me. Now I'm invisible
with looking for you, cataloguing nights
to turn up the one memory
which will attract you back into my life,
I have the need to reinforce a day
in summer, fried seaweed, we found a pool
commandeered by an olive crab which moved
bluntly from stone to stone, and never spoke
about that other tilt of consciousness –
the things not understood by speech,
and lost the moment to fill in ourselves
with the unapprehended shadow side
I live with now, and your torn fishnet tights
crumple to diamonds within easy reach.

BURNT PAGES

Last night, she stood naked against a tree,
skin rubbed by the bark's ribbed asperity
and listened out for owls: oval chuckles,
voice effects in the thicket. He was there,
draped in an old third Reichstag flag,
pretending he was someone else, and ran
the length of the white road with outstretched
                                        hands,
and came back days later, she never knew
what he intended by this blank
or where he went with the power turned up
and open-ended in the dark. The dark
inhabited by blood-bibbed owls, etc.

She concentrates hard on her life,
or rather on its absence; she can't touch
or stop the process, halt it like a film,
freezing the right moment to permanence.
She'd have an interlude, a sunlit gap
in which to be. A loghouse in the woods,
an orange painted bench outside.
Instead, she settles to extending time
by adopting roles, and tonight elects
to dress in silver, party in a flat
with new utopians, discover a lead
to islands, pink coral beaches,
the private aircraft touching down on sand,

a timeless zone, no other occupants
but one bug-eyed, antennae raised, gold cat.

EQUAL TO FANTASY

I hunt the image through an afternoon,
obsessed, distracted, looking for someone
I'll recognize, the face I saw and lost
in such a street as this, a mauve jumper
swallowed by an alley, I went on back
a thousand times, as I return today
appropriating what I'll use
for poetry, riffling through magazines
in Old Compton Street, and the model's eyes
are green ovals beneath an architrave
on which a lion swallows a gold sun.
Her dress is a silk felt-tip on the skin.
I go back to my search, imagining
I'll walk clean through a blue mirror
into the clear zone, it's a loop-shaped park
in which I see her in a mauve jumper
walking from sunlight to shadow,
the two lie as distinct striped parallels
across the grass. When I call out to her
she seems equal to my request,
as though she's tapped into my needs for months,
and comes towards me. We will never meet
without a quantum leap out of dream-time.
I hurry on, someone scanning the crowd
with a visible, desperate need
to find the image, meet my completion,
and break a window to the other side.

DIRECT TO THE STARS

His fingers drum-taps for the waiting vowels
to shiver on the page. She builds her hair
to a rococo construct, sticks a pin,
a second, has the build up hold.
He lives with water buffalo
breasting the current as he writes, hot breath
steaming as vision on the river bank.
The scene changes to a small hotel room,
his blue shirt, her blue dress over a chair,
and for some reason a mango
is centred on the bed. Its blotchy skin
is coloured like a parakeet. A flick
and he's in Casablanca. A white heat
fizzes like a lozenge in the white sky.
She really goes outside and comes back in
her arms full of bright towels, the washed out jeans
she'll wear this afternoon. She smells of sun.
He likes to kiss the light out of her mouth.
He gets back to the water buffalo.
They lie down in the shade. It's afternoon
inside the poem too. One of them rolls
a lazy head, then tenses on the spot.
He travels further with the herd, and soon
it's evening, and she sits outside,
the pressed jeans moulded to her, and still hot.

THE GOLD LODGE IN THE EAST PARK

An hour a day she's on the balcony
and blowy leaf shadows splash big tattoos
over the gaps her silver bikini
make evident. A helicopter's props
mash through the afternoon. She turns over
and reads face own, a parallel tangent
that takes her to an alley in Venice,
a dragon figurehead's above a door,
the air's fuzzy with rain – it's almost night,
and upstairs, the two of them can't delay,
passports, the airport. The crime's near perfect,
the body stored in liquid nitrogen
6,000 miles away, to be revived
later without the memory of death.
She reads, then stands up topless. He is there,

the man who comes back each afternoon and waits
to the left of the house. She doesn't know
the exact plane of his reality,
he's always dressed in black, with blue glasses,
she never properly sees his face,
but is compelled to wait for him each day
and live the chemical high they transfer
by inner gestures. Even in the cold,
he stands there breath smoking, always on time
at half past three. Tomorrow she'll wear gold,
the next day black. Today, he waves a hand,
and she knows if she asks him up, she'll find

star-maps written beneath his feet,
his guide to origins, and now a mist
blows like white curlicues across the heat.

WHERE SHE IS WHERE IS SHE

The days drop down exhausted like dead birds.
I look for autumn in the spring,
your red skirt redder than a dahlia,
electrifies my fingers on contact,
riffling the second skins in your wardrobe,
memories burning in my eye,
demanding I go out into the street
and search for you, and look again, again
returning inconsolably
to things I do not like, the empty flat,
the night filling with exacting preludes
to storm and self-estrangement, dilemma
I can't release, nor hope to relocate
a memory that comforts. I lose out
to spontaneity, miss how my life
should free-associate with accidents,
disturb brightly coloured clouds from my hands,
a nut-brown creature from the apple's core.
Instead, I telescope into the past,
repossess every memory,
speak to your absence, peel a red orange
to taste sharpness at the interior,
my tongue dipped in a sweetness which won't last.

WHITE NIGHTS

Those nights, the white ones in between the black,
the special interludes, when dream translates
into sustained reality,
implosive cocktails shooting in his blood,
images blazing out like close up stars,
he recollects their cool burning, the red
jacket he drapes to walk the lawn
amazed, expecting screen words in the sky,
his past on spontaneous recall,
light frequencies reinventing colours,
a bridge slung right across the horizon
on which a young girl riding a tiger
is pursued by a flashback from childhood,
himself stalking her through an afternoon
of autumn fires, ruby bangs on shook trees,
he lives intensely then, and dreams all day
of what he's seen. The build-up buzzes now,
as though a drug-clip fed speed to his veins,
and he prepares for vision, makes contact
with the nightside of things, the brighter light
in which he goes to meet the universe
the photons punching like hologram bees.

HIGHROAD TO BLACK CHASM FALLS

A dark blue rainbow stands up vertical,
a telescopic trail to the image
that's fractionally elusive, tilting wide
like a green paintpot balanced on a cloud.
He kills the car and sits there in the still,
and big scenes from his past come tumbling by,
amazing captions fractured by the speed
at which they build towards no end,
like clouds heading somewhere we never see,
but keep as abstract. He can hear the falls
audibly fanning out. The sound's a bee
trapped in a bottle in a dream,
the glass shattered on waking. Who were they,
the couple disappearing down the road,
her white skirt floating, and the way they walked
gave him an extra hand behind his back?
They came from nowhere, never looked around,
but were part of a journey. He leans back,
a single elongated drip
of green paint smudges on a heavy cloud.
He can't connect with the centrality,
but just the residue, the indirect
leakage from image. He kicks the car fast
into a dust-cloud, overtakes the two,
they wave to see him go, and white vapour
hangs like steam-bath in the dazzled air.

J.R.R. Tolkien
The Books, The Films, The Whole Cultural Phenomenon

by Jeremy Mark Robinson

A new critical study of J.R.R. Tolkien, creator of Middle-earth and author of *The Lord of the Rings, The Hobbit* and *The Silmarillion*, among other books.

This new critical study explores Tolkien's major writings (*The Lord of the Rings, The Hobbit, Beowulf: The Monster and the Critics, The Letters, The Silmarillion* and *The History of Middle-earth* volumes); Tolkien and fairy tales; the mythological, political and religious aspects of Tolkien's Middle-earth; the critics' response to Tolkien's fiction over the decades; the Tolkien industry (merchandizing, toys, role-playing games, posters, Tolkien societies, conferences and the like); Tolkien in visual and fantasy art; the cultural aspects of The Lord of the Rings (from the 1950s to the present); Tolkien's fiction's relationship with other fantasy fiction, such as C.S. Lewis and *Harry Potter*; and the TV, radio and film versions of Tolkien's books, including the 2001-03 Hollywood interpretations of *The Lord of the Rings*.

This new book draws on contemporary cultural theory and analysis and offers a sympathetic and illuminating (and sceptical) account of the Tolkien phenomenon. This book is designed to appeal to the general reader (and viewer) of Tolkien: it is written in a clear, jargon-free and easily-accessible style.

754pp   ISBN 1-86171-057-7   £25.00 / $37.50

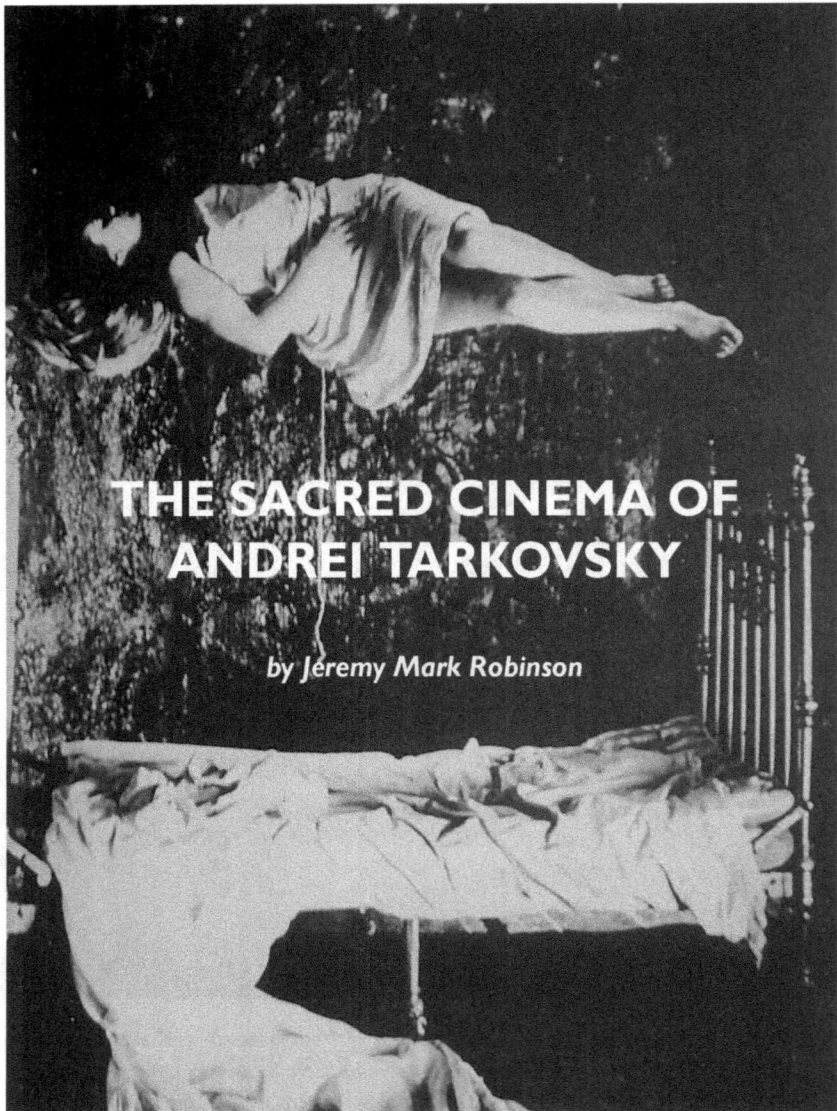

THE SACRED CINEMA OF
ANDREI TARKOVSKY

by Jeremy Mark Robinson

A new study of the Russian filmmaker Andrei Tarkovsky (1932-1986), director of seven feature films, including *Andrei Roublyov, Mirror, Solaris, Stalker* and *The Sacrifice*.
This is one of the most comprehensive and detailed studies of Tarkovsky's cinema available. Every film is explored in depth, with scene-by-scene analyses. All aspects of Tarkovsky's output are critiqued, including editing, camera, staging, script, budget, collaborations, production, sound, music, performance and spirituality. Tarkovsky is placed with a European New Wave tradition of filmmaking, alongside directors like Ingmar Bergman, Carl Theodor Dreyer, Pier Paolo Pasolini and Robert Bresson.
An essential addition to film studies.

Illustrations: 150 b/w, 4 colour. 682 pages. First edition. Hardback.

Publisher: Crescent Moon Publishing. Distributor: Gardners Books.

ISBN 1-86171-096-8 (9781861710963) £60.00 / $105.00

The Best of Peter Redgrove's Poetry
The Book of Wonders

by Peter Redgrove, edited and introduced by Jeremy Robinson

Poems of wet shirts and 'wonder-awakening dresses'; honey, wasps and bees; orchards and apples; rivers, seas and tides; storms, rain, weather and clouds; waterworks; labyrinths; amazing perfumes; the Cornish landscape (Penzance, Perranporth, Falmouth, Boscastle, the Lizard and Scilly Isles); the sixth sense and 'extra-sensuous perception'; witchcraft; alchemical vessels and laboratories; yoga; menstruation; mines, minerals and stones; sand dunes; mud-baths; mythology; dreaming; vulvas; and lots of sex magic. This book gathers together poetry (and prose) from every stage of Redgrove's career, and every book. It includes pieces that have only appeared in small presses and magazines, and in uncollected form.

'Peter Redgrove is really an extraordinary poet' (George Szirtes, *Quarto* magazine) 'Peter Redgrove is one of the few significant poets now writing... His 'means' are indeed brilliant and delightful. Technically he is a poet essentially of brilliant and unexpected images...he never disappoints' (Kathleen Raine, *Temenos* magazine).

240pp   ISBN 1-86171-063-1   2nd edition   £19.99 / $29.50

Sex–Magic–Poetry–Cornwall
A Flood of Poems

by Peter Redgrove. Edited with an essay by Jeremy Robinson

A marvellous collection of poems by one of Britain's best but underrated poets, Peter Redgrove. This book brings together some of Redgrove's wildest and most passionate works, creating a 'flood' of poetry. Philip Hobsbaum called Redgrove 'the great poet of our time', while Angela Carter said: 'Redgrove's language can light up a page.' Redgrove ranks alongside Ted Hughes and Sylvia Plath. He is in every way a 'major poet'. Robinson's essay analyzes all of Redgrove's poetic work, including his use of sex magic, natural science, menstruation, psychology, myth, alchemy and feminism.
A new edition, including a new introduction, new preface and new bibliography.

'Robinson's enthusiasm is winning, and his perceptive readings are supported by a very useful bibliography' (*Acumen* magazine)
'*Sex-Magic-Poetry-Cornwall* is a very rich essay... It is like a brightly-lighted box. (Peter Redgrove)
'This is an excellent selection of poetry and an extensive essay on the themes and theories of this unusual poet by Jeremy Robinson' (*Chapman* magazine)

220pp   New, 3rd edition   ISBN 1-86171-070-4   £14.99 / $23.50

THE ART OF
ANDY GOLDSWORTHY

COMPLETE WORKS: SPECIAL EDITION
(PAPERBACK and HARDBACK)

by William Malpas

A new, special edition of the study of the contemporary British sculptor,
Andy Goldsworthy, including a new introduction, new bibliography and many
new illustrations.

This is the most comprehensive, up-to-date, well-researched and in-depth
account of Goldsworthy's art available anywhere.

Andy Goldsworthy makes land art. His sculpture is a sensitive, intuitive
response to nature, light, time, growth, the seasons and the earth. Goldswor-
thy's environmental art is becoming ever more popular: 1993's art book
Stone was a bestseller; the press raved about Goldsworthy taking over a
number of London West End art galleries in 1994; during 1995 Goldsworthy
designed a set of Royal Mail stamps and had a show at the British Museum.
Malpas surveys all of Goldsworthy's art, and analyzes his relation with other
land artists such as Robert Smithson, Walter de Maria, Richard Long and
David Nash, and his place in the contemporary British art scene.

The Art of Andy Goldsworthy discusses all of Goldsworthy's important and
recent exhibitions and books, including the *Sheepfolds* project; the TV docu-
mentaries; *Wood* (1996); the New York Holocaust memorial (2003); and
Goldsworthy's collaboration on a dance performance.

Illustrations: 70 b/w, 1 colour. 330 pages. New, special, 2nd edition.
Publisher: Crescent Moon Publishing. Distributor: Gardners Books.

ISBN 1-86171-059-3 (9781861710598) (Paperback) £25.00 / $44.00

ISBN 1-86171-080-1 (9781861710802) (Hardback) £60.00 / $105.00

CRESCENT MOON PUBLISHING

ARTS, PAINTING, SCULPTURE

The Art of Andy Goldsworthy: Complete Works(Pbk)
The Art of Andy Goldsworthy: Complete Works (Hbk)
Andy Goldsworthy in Close-Up (Pbk)
Andy Goldsworthy in Close-Up (Hbk)
Land Art: A Complete Guide
Richard Long: The Art of Walking
The Art of Richard Long: Complete Works (Pbk)
The Art of Richard Long: Complete Works (Hbk)
Richard Long in Close-Up
Land Art In the UK
Land Art in Close-Up
Installation Art in Close-Up
Minimal Art and Artists In the 1960s and After
Colourfield Painting
Land Art DVD, TV documentary
Andy Goldsworthy DVD, TV documentary
The Erotic Object: Sexuality in Sculpture From Prehistory to the Present Day
Sex in Art: Pornography and Pleasure in Painting and Sculpture
Postwar Art
Sacred Gardens: The Garden in Myth, Religion and Art
Glorification: Religious Abstraction in Renaissance and 20th Century Art
Early Netherlandish Painting
Leonardo da Vinci
Piero della Francesca
Giovanni Bellini
Fra Angelico: Art and Religion in the Renaissance
Mark Rothko: The Art of Transcendence
Frank Stella: American Abstract Artist
Jasper Johns: Painting By Numbers
Brice Marden
Alison Wilding: The Embrace of Sculpture
Vincent van Gogh: Visionary Landscapes
Eric Gill: Nuptials of God
Constantin Brancusi: Sculpting the Essence of Things
Max Beckmann
Egon Schiele: Sex and Death In Purple Stockings
Delizioso Fotografico Fervore: Works In Process 1
Sacro Cuore: Works In Process 2
The Light Eternal: J.M.W. Turner
The Madonna Glorified: Karen Arthurs

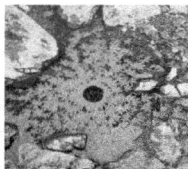

LITERATURE

J.R.R. Tolkien: The Books, The Films, The Whole Cultural Phenomenon
Harry Potter
Sexing Hardy: Thomas Hardy and Feminism
Thomas Hardy's *Tess of the d'Urbervilles*
Thomas Hardy's *Jude the Obscure*
Thomas Hardy: The Tragic Novels
Love and Tragedy: Thomas Hardy
The Poetry of Landscape in Hardy
Wessex Revisited: Thomas Hardy and John Cowper Powys
Wolfgang Iser: Essays
Petrarch, Dante and the Troubadours
Maurice Sendak and the Art of Children's Book Illustration
Andrea Dworkin
Cixous, Irigaray, Kristeva: The *Jouissance* of French Feminism
Julia Kristeva: Art, Love, Melancholy, Philosophy, Semiotics and Psychoanalysis
Hélène Cixous I Love You: The *Jouissance* of Writing
Luce Irigaray: Lips, Kissing, and the Politics of Sexual Difference
Peter Redgrove: Here Comes the Flood
Peter Redgrove: Sex-Magic-Poetry-Cornwall
Lawrence Durrell: Between Love and Death, East and West
Love, Culture & Poetry: Lawrence Durrell
Cavafy: Anatomy of a Soul
German Romantic Poetry: Goethe, Novalis, Heine, Hölderlin, Schlegel, Schiller
Feminism and Shakespeare
Shakespeare: Selected Sonnets
Shakespeare: Love, Poetry & Magic
The Passion of D.H. Lawrence
D.H. Lawrence: Symbolic Landscapes
D.H. Lawrence: Infinite Sensual Violence
Rimbaud: Arthur Rimbaud and the Magic of Poetry
The Ecstasies of John Cowper Powys
Sensualism and Mythology: The Wessex Novels of John Cowper Powys
Amorous Life: John Cowper Powys and the Manifestation of Affectivity (H.W. Fawkner)
Postmodern Powys: New Essays on John Cowper Powys (Joe Boulter)
Rethinking Powys: Critical Essays on John Cowper Powys
Paul Bowles & Bernardo Bertolucci
Rainer Maria Rilke
In the Dim Void: Samuel Beckett
Samuel Beckett Goes into the Silence
André Gide: Fiction and Fervour
Jackie Collins and the Blockbuster Novel
Blinded By Her Light: The Love-Poetry of Robert Graves
The Passion of Colours: Travels In Mediterranean Lands
Poetic Forms
The Dolphin-Boy

POETRY

The Best of Peter Redgrove's Poetry
Peter Redgrove: Here Comes The Flood
Peter Redgrove: Sex-Magic-Poetry-Cornwall
Ursula Le Guin: Walking In Cornwall
Dante: Selections From the Vita Nuova
Petrarch, Dante and the Troubadours
William Shakespeare: Selected Sonnets
Blinded By Her Light: The Love-Poetry of Robert Graves
Emily Dickinson: Selected Poems
Emily Brontë: Poems
Thomas Hardy: Selected Poems
Percy Bysshe Shelley: Poems
John Keats: Selected Poems
D.H. Lawrence: Selected Poems
Edmund Spenser: Poems
John Donne: Poems
Henry Vaughan: Poems
Sir Thomas Wyatt: Poems
Robert Herrick: Selected Poems
Rilke: Space, Essence and Angels in the Poetry of Rainer Maria Rilke
Rainer Maria Rilke: Selected Poems
Friedrich Hölderlin: Selected Poems
Arseny Tarkovsky: Selected Poems
Arthur Rimbaud: Selected Poems
Arthur Rimbaud: A Season in Hell
Arthur Rimbaud and the Magic of Poetry
D.J. Enright: By-Blows
Jeremy Reed: Brigitte's Blue Heart
Jeremy Reed: Claudia Schiffer's Red Shoes
Gorgeous Little Orpheus
Radiance: New Poems
Crescent Moon Book of Nature Poetry
Crescent Moon Book of Love Poetry
Crescent Moon Book of Mystical Poetry
Crescent Moon Book of Elizabethan Love Poetry
Crescent Moon Book of Metaphysical Poetry
Crescent Moon Book of Romantic Poetry
Pagan America: New American Poetry

MEDIA, CINEMA, FEMINISM and CULTURAL STUDIES

J.R.R. Tolkien: The Books, The Films, The Whole Cultural Phenomenon
Harry Potter
Cixous, Irigaray, Kristeva: The *Jouissance* of French Feminism
Julia Kristeva: Art, Love, Melancholy, Philosophy, Semiotics and   Psychoanalysis
Luce Irigaray: Lips, Kissing, and the Politics of Sexual Difference
Hélene Cixous I Love You: The *Jouissance* of Writing
Andrea Dworkin
'Cosmo Woman': The World of Women's Magazines
Women in Pop Music
Discovering the Goddess (Geoffrey Ashe)
The Poetry of Cinema
The Sacred Cinema of Andrei Tarkovsky (Pbk and Hbk)
Paul Bowles & Bernardo Bertolucci
Media Hell: Radio, TV and the Press
An Open Letter to the BBC
Detonation Britain: Nuclear War in the UK
Feminism and Shakespeare
Wild Zones: Pornography, Art and Feminism
Sex in Art: Pornography and Pleasure in Painting and Sculpture
Sexing Hardy: Thomas Hardy and Feminism

In my view *The Light Eternal* is among the very best of all the material I read on Turner. (Douglas Graham, director of the Turner Museum, Denver, Colorado)

The Light Eternal is a model monograph, an exemplary job. The subject matter of the book is beautifully organised and dead on beam. (Lawrence Durrell)

It is amazing for me to see my work treated with such passion and respect. (Andrea Dworkin)

Sex-Magic-Poetry-Cornwall is a very rich essay... It is like a brightly-lighted box. (Peter Redgrove)

CRESCENT MOON PUBLISHING
P.O. Box 393, Maidstone, Kent, ME14 5XU, United Kingdom.
01622-729593 (UK) 01144-1622-729593 (US) 0044-1622-729593 (other territories)
cresmopub@yahoo.co.uk   www.crescentmoon.org.uk